# YOGA for Beginners

Discover and Learn How Less Than 15 Minutes of Yoga a Day can Transform your Life Eternally. Included Precise, Illustrated Postures and Sequences.

GW00467597

Viola Evans

"Yoga is the journey of the self, through the self,

to the self"

The Bhagavad Gita

**Yoga by Evans**

TIME, SPACE, EQUILIBRIUM. IN HARMONY WITH YOUR LIFE

# Table of Contents

# About the Author

Hi, I'm Viola.

Thank you very much for purchasing my book.

In this book, we are going to go through a small path. The purpose is to give you a greater awareness of yourself and what you can achieve with Yoga.

Yoga is pure magic, something that we feel inside our body and that manifests more or less intensely outside of it.

When you start doing Yoga, don't immediately focus on the physical mechanisms or the technical aspect; instead, think about the energetic impulses you receive from your body.

Every yoga session always begins by listening to and feeling your breath. This immediately makes you realize that Yoga is part of you.

In fact, a good instructor must make you grasp this aspect of Yoga.


If you have the pleasure and interest in staying up to date with the world of Yoga, you can subscribe to my community for free. I do not send spam, and your email address is not shared with anyone.

Every week, I will send you an email where you can read about simple posture sequences to improve your mood and start your days off right.

To subscribe, frame this QR code with your smartphone; you will be directed to an Internet page of mine.

Now, happy reading and happy Yoga.

# Introduction

Have you ever wondered about the history of yoga? Its origins are very ancient: the earliest traces of the practice date from between 3000 and 1800 BEC. in the Indus Valley, in the peasant civilization of Quetta, and later in the towns of Harappa and Mohenjo Daro.

In excavations in these areas, statuettes and depictions seated in yogic positions have been found, probably showing how yoga was already known and practiced then.

However, the first clear traces of yoga come to us from a later period, that of Vedic literature. The Vedas are very ancient texts whose contents were handed down from generation to generation through oral tradition before being outlined in literary form. There is not yet a precise elaboration of yoga in the Vedas, but some yogic concepts have already appeared.

We can find the foundations of yoga in the final and later part of the Vedas. In the Upanishads, philosophical-religious texts were written in Sanskrit between 800 and 300 B.C. In some passages, topics such as Prana, vital energy, and Nadi, energy pathways, are dealt with, which will later be central themes in Hatha-yoga. That is a form of yoga based on psychophysical exercises that teach how to master the cosmic energy present in man. Finally, the Svatasvatara Upanishad describes yogic practices and their effects.

In the epic period (dating from about the sixth century B.C.), a rich source for understanding yoga is the Mahabharata, the most essential part of which is the Bhagavadgita.

This treatise of seven hundred verses summarizes various yoga ideas and practices, defining three of the most critical "ways": Karma yoga, the way of action; Bhakti yoga, the method of devotion; and Jnana yoga, the way of knowledge.

The next period is the Sutras (2nd century B.C. to 4th century A.D.). Sutra is a very concise form of literature: short sentences expound concepts and ideas in essential words. In addition, the structure of the sutras allowed for memorization of the entire teaching. Among the most important are the Yoga Sutras of Patanjali, a second-century BCE philosopher. These were interpreted by different commentators who developed the concepts according to other currents of thought.

In the medieval period, the predominant literature is that of the Tantras. Many of the practices of Hatha-yoga seem to have originated in the literature of the Tantras.

Some of the most essential Hatha-yoga texts are the Hathayogapradipika, the Gheranda Samhita, and the Siva.

Samhita. In modern times important yoga masters have been Swami Vivekananda, Yogananda Paramahansa, Sri Aurobindo, Ramana Maharshi, and Swami Sivananda.

# What is Yoga?

Yoga is an ancient discipline based on a unified body, mind, and spirit development system. Yoga means "union" and is derived from the Sanskrit root "Yuji," indicating the opposite entities' physical and spiritual union. Body and mind, stillness and movement, male and female, and sun and moon are some of the opposites that the practice of Yoga aspires to bring together. The ultimate goal is to get a peaceful and deep reconciliation.

Yoga is not a technique, not limited to the performance of postures or breathing exercises, but, through them, acts on a deeper level whose goal is the union between body and mind, between the individual and universal consciousness.

The benefits derived from Yoga are only partly physical in nature but primarily mental. In fact, constant practice increases self-awareness. Moreover, as shown by many studies, it gives a sense of calm and general well-being, promoting this discipline in private life and in the workplace or recovery programs.

Yoga is a path to spirituality and the attainment of inner peace and happiness, so much so that Patanjali, in his "Yoga Sutra," one of the most essential texts in classical Yoga, organizes this path into eight stages or eight branches:

1.    Yama (universal ethical and moral principles)
2.    Niyama (personal guidelines)
3.    Asana (postures)
4.    Pranayama (breath control)

5.      Pratyahara (retraction of the senses)

6.      Dharana (concentration)

7.      Dhyana (meditation)

8.      Samadhi (state of grace, contemplation)

## Yoga today

Today's term yoga refers to a vast range of conceptions and practices. Although it has its roots in the Indian tradition, yoga has, over time, transcended the geographical and cultural boundaries of India, integrating with different philosophies: traditions such as Tibetan yoga, Taoist, Buddhist, and others have developed. The practice is suitable for everyone, adults, seniors, and even children

# History of yoga

## Ashtanga

This is a very famous and practiced style of yoga that aims to lead the practitioner toward gradual self-awareness. Literally, the word Ashtanga means the number 8. It represents the 8 levels of yoga practice described by Patanjali: these levels are Yama (abstinence), Nyama (fulfillment), Asana (postures), Pranayama (Breath Control), Pratyahara (sense control), Dharana (concentration), Dhyana (meditation), and Samadhi (contemplation). Ashtanga Yoga was developed by Guru Tirumala Krishnamacharya in India. He opened the first school dedicated to it to spread this style to the public. The practice involves 6 different sets of postures. The asanas are repeated in a specific order, from the most straightforward set to the most psychophysically demanding.

The foundation of this practice is the breath, which is always synchronized with the body's movements: the recovery of proper breathing improves blood circulation and bodily functions.

## Kundalini

Also widely known and practiced, this is a yogic style that aims to awaken kundalini energy, often graphically represented as a coiled snake at the base of the spine. Literally, the term is derived from kundal, meaning curl, and ini, meaning feminine energy. The goal is to improve the body's mental and physical balance through physical exercises and meditations.

Kundalini yoga has its roots in Vedic texts. It is part of the currents of Hatha, Raja, Laya, and Mantra yoga of the so-called tantric yoga. The practice is structured in "classes," i.e., classes that from time-to-time work on a specific body chakra (energy center) and may also be different depending on the season of the year. Unlike Ashtanga yoga, Kundalini yoga has no set sequence.

## Hatha

Hatha yoga, perhaps the most famous of all styles, aims to improve the elasticity of the body and spine through the practice of meditation, breath (pranayama), and asanas. Hatha yoga is often translated as the yoga of effort or strength because of the practice's, particularly challenging positions. The origins date back to the writing of the early Tantras. At the same time, the arrangement of the method is due to the mystic Gorakhnath, who lived between the 11th and 12th centuries. Precisely because of the complexity of its exercises. Hatha yoga is indicated to restore elasticity to muscles and tendons and prevent and treat back pain.

# Styles of Yoga

There are different styles of Yoga, from fast-paced and vigorous or very gentle and slow-paced. All types of Yoga provide benefits, but it is essential to assess your needs to choose the proper practice.

Hatha Yoga Ha = solar, Tha = lunar, which can mean restoring mental and physical balance and the union of body, mind, and spirit. Fundamentals and postural alignments essential to the practice of asanas (postures) are taught. Emphasis is placed on core strength, flexibility, balance, concentration, and breath awareness.

Vinyasa is a Sanskrit term often used to describe various yoga styles. The word Vinyasa can be decoded from its root Nyasa "to place" and Vi "in a special way." It symbolizes a dynamic and fluid form of Yoga. Postures are linked together using the breath in a sustained and vigorous rhythm. This style originated in the Ashtanga Vinyasa Yoga of Sri Tirumala Krishnamacharya, a master of Pattabhi Jois. They applied the principles of breathing to the Vinyasa yoga form. Like all styles of yoga, Vinyasa has both physical and mental benefits. Physically, sweat expels toxins by regenerating the body. The synchronized breath relaxes the mind and helps release energy blockages throughout the body. Recommended for those who have already mastered basic yoga principles.

Hatha Flow is a dynamic series of postures using breath in harmony with movement. Holding asanas and caring for alignment are fundamental principles of this practice. Transitions from one pose to another occur by following the flow of the breath in respect of mindful movement. Students learn to specify postures and move beyond the limitations of the body-mind in a kind of moving meditation.

Gentle flow is a gentle yoga that combines postures/asanas into a fluid, meditative practice. It is perfect for beginner and advanced students to welcome soft openings and increased body-mind awareness. In addition, it is recommended for those who prefer a less vigorous practice, those experiencing times of particular stress and fatigue, those recovering after convalescence, and those returning to physical activity after a long time. Yin Yoga is a slow style of Yoga that incorporates the principles of traditional Chinese medicine, with asanas (postures) that are held for more extended periods than other styles, averaging 2 to 5 minutes. Yin sequences are intended to stimulate the channels of the subtle body, known as "meridians" in Chinese medicine and as "nadis" in Hatha Yoga. Yin yoga postures apply moderate stress to the body's connective tissues (tendons, fascia, and ligaments) to increase circulation in the joints and improve flexibility. A more meditative approach to Yoga, its goals are awareness of inner silence and bringing to light a universal quality of interconnectedness. Because this practice often includes several seated postures and forward bends, it also restores energy and calms the nervous system.

Restorative Yoga consists of a series of postures asanas supported by tools (blankets, pillows, bricks, straps) and held for several minutes. The body receives support through these supports, can relax, and gently let's go. These forms allow deep physical, mental and emotional relaxation by activating the parasympathetic nervous system.

Through Restorative Yoga, the body is regenerated, aligned, and rebalanced.

It is recommended for those suffering from stress disorders, hypertension, anxiety, insomnia, muscle tension, motor difficulties related to post-surgery therapy, and anyone who wants to learn how to relax. Hot Stone Restorative during these deep rest positions, a few heated basalt stones are gently placed on the body over the clothing. The heat from the stones gently penetrates the muscles, melting away layers of physical and emotional tension and promoting relaxation.

Yoga in Pregnancy is an energizing, gentle flow adapted for pregnant women that promotes stability, flexibility, and vitality. This class offers mothers a space to relax and connect with themselves. It is excellent preparation for childbirth through breath and mind-body awareness.

Postnatal Yoga supports the new mother from a physical point of view to regain muscle tone and mobility and from an emotional point of view by providing the tools to face the new parental role with serenity. A gentle practice that helps regain balance in body and mind. A space to take care of oneself, relax, strengthen the bond with the baby and share the experience with other new mothers. For babies from 40 days up to the ninth month of age (pre-baby).

Alignment Our bodies are dynamic entities. A healthy body can respond to changes that occur day by day. Proper alignment allows the natural flow of fluids and breath, supporting the functioning of the nervous system. In this class, we refine inner perception in dialogue with outer perception, working on alignment and mobility of the spine.

Through stretching, mobilization, micro, and macro movement practices, with the help of breath, imagination, and visualization, we make our central line, fulcrum, and axis of life malleable and strong.

The proposed work is an excellent preparation for the Yoga practice of asanas/postures: the root "as" means to sit royally, i.e., with the spine extended.

Pranayama and Meditation A class devoted to breathing practice and silent listening. Pranayama: Prana = breath, energy, life, strength - Yama = expand, control, stop, direct. It is a process of expanding our habitual reserve of Prana through extending, directing, and regulating the breath. We warm up with a series of stretches and preparatory asanas to open the breathing muscles. The middle part of the path is devoted to breathing with preparatory exercises proceeding to the practice of Pranayama. It concludes with a final meditation and relaxation.

Meditation Yoga aspires to the union of mind and body through physical practice and awareness of the senses. While practicing Yoga, one meditates through the exercise of moving presence. Seated meditation is silent and compassionate listening to the self, is a purification of the mind, and can promote self-acceptance, exploration, awareness, mind-body balance, and compassion. It can help those suffering from anxiety, stress, depression, and trauma.

# Benefits of yoga

There is much more to yoga than what the eyes see. The benefits and effects of yoga on an individual are much more than physical change, a flexible body, and toned muscles. Flexibility and strength in life off the mat are also and, more importantly, manifested. What is experienced on the mat is learned and begins to be learned off the mat? Yoga is the art of learning more and more about oneself and others and putting it into practice to improve oneself. Yoga is a "martial" art that helps in life's daily challenges.

# Psychological benefits

In the practice of asana, pranayama, and meditation, the effect is immediate. One feels better, calmer, more stable, and has more flexible mood swings. As the months go by, one discovers a change in point of view; one accepts the present more and feels more gratitude. Opening one's eyes to a much broader perspective. Yoga teaches that we are all different and we are all the same. In this view, each person in particular, and each person is unique and, because of that, excellent.

So, it is not just physical practice on the mat, but it enters into life without even realizing it. There are indeed numerous psychological benefits of yoga. The body and mind react spontaneously, and we often notice the result and effects only after a long time. But what changes and how the body responds starts from the first class.

## Scientific Benefits

For many years now, science has proven that yoga is good for the body and mind and helps alleviate many chronic symptoms. Among the many studies carried out, we report research from the Erasmus University Medical Center in Rotterdam that yoga helps protect against the risk of heart disease and that metabolic syndrome.

In fact, it was found that those who practice yoga have a lower risk of obesity, high blood pressure, and high cholesterol. How so? The reason is immediately stated: asanas that develop strength and flexibility and improve breathing reduces blood pressure.

Recall also that yoga is effective against headaches, insomnia, and menstrual pain. It also prevents many of the typical discomforts of menopause.

## Benefits in the short term

What happens after a yoga class?

- concentration increases.
- stress is reduced.

- stiffness of the body decreases.

- increases flexibility.

- brain functions such as memory and learning ability improve.

- the body relaxes.

- the heartbeats lighter.

When you begin to notice that going to yoga class feels good, the consistency and weekly participation often make you yearn for the next class, and you begin to see more and more effects.

## Benefits in the medium term

After a few months of practice, yoga gives much more:

- rebalances blood pressure.

- improves lung capacity to breathe more deeply.

- improves sexuality by helping to solve problems related to the reproductive system.

- reduces chronic pain and back pain.

- decreases anxiety and depression.

- improves balance.

- the nervous system improves its functions by calming the body and physical tension.

- glands reduce the production of cortisol, the stress hormone that causes junk food cravings.

- muscles become more toned.

- the abdomen is refined as each position uses the abdominal muscles (read here: how to develop abdominals with yoga), losing the belly fat that builds up, helping to lose inches at the waist center.

- it improves flexibility by getting to be able to perform postures that were previously inaccessible.

- virtues such as calmness and patience are strengthened.

- body perception improves by paying more attention to what you eat.

- the body becomes stronger and cleaner, inside and out.

- it helps with discipline.

## Long-term benefits

After a few years of yoga, the practice helps improve in every respect the performance of the body and mind with many other tremendous benefits:

- a steady weight is achieved without exaggerated swaying.

- bones become more muscular, decreasing the risk of osteoporosis and arthritis.

- it decreases the risk of disease.

- reduces heart issues.

- the brain gains more control over fear and anger.

- you learn to let go of what no longer serves you, both on a physical level by moving into asana more deeply each day and off the mat by letting go of stress and unpleasant emotions.

- the message that results from asanas on the organs gives an organism that is renewed and rejuvenated every day.

- the energy and positive vibration that are transmitted are also felt by others.

There are many benefits of yoga, so it is very often recommended by doctors as an integral part of therapy and healing. By the way, yoga is for everyone, and everyone can benefit from it. So, whether it's just to move around a bit, recover from physical or emotional trauma, or lose weight- no matter who you are or what reason you get on the mat, the benefits are assured.

# Hormonal yoga

## What is hormonal yoga?

Hormone yoga is a technique that works on hormone production by stimulating the glands.

*Dinah Rodrigues*, a psychologist and yoga teacher, explains that her hormone yoga therapy technique was explicitly created to prevent and relieve menopausal symptoms. Different than hatha yoga, hormone yoga is:

- therapeutic
- dynamic
- based on physiology.

Dinah Rodrigues devised an Asana sequence based on female physiology, indicating against the declining function of hormone-producing glands.

For this reason, Rodrigues' exercises are ideal for menopausal women. With an internal massage, hormone yoga positions stimulate the ovaries, adrenal glands, pituitary gland, and thyroid gland.

You can reactivate hormone production and immediately begin a rejuvenation process through this practice. Yoga, designed by the Brazilian teacher, works on the health of the body, thanks to its dynamic technique, and on the mind, helping you find balance.

Dynamic yoga exercises increase organ and gland function and strengthen the effect of postures (asana) and breathing techniques (pranayama) through Tibetan energy principles. The purpose of hormone yoga therapy is to practice internal massage through:

- Dynamic Asanas
- Deep Pranayama
- methodical and continuous practice

With a regular and consistent program that reactivates hormone production and stimulates your vitality and mental and physical balance, you will succeed in flourishing again.

Fight the symptoms of menopause through a safe and certified method. Resurge in change and discover all the opportunities this period can give you.

## How hormone yoga is practiced

Hormone yoga therapy (HYT) involves exercises that are simple to perform. It is designed for women's health as they go through the changing phase of menopause and want to see results in their bodies and mood.

Even after a short course with a certified HYT teacher, you can start practicing the activity independently and observe the first results. This activity initially helps you create a new phase of life a lot.

By following Rodrigues' method consistently, you can soon see results on physical appearance, but how do the exercises work? The asana sequence provided is to stimulate the ovaries with a massage.

It starts from a comfortable position and involves asanas that follow one another smoothly, deep breathing, and visualization exercises. Asana and pranayama increase the function of the glands. At the same time, visualization of the result works as a powerful motivator. It gives you the correct charge to follow the method consistently.

Hormone yoga should be practiced four times a week in half-hour sessions. To see the effects on hormone levels, it is vital to incorporate it into a lifestyle that includes every aspect of your life, from nutrition to exercise. In addition, you must base your results on precise data that will give you the drive to continue taking care of yourself.

Fight menopause symptoms through a safe and certified method. Then, resurface in change and discover all the opportunities this period can give you.

## The benefits of hormonal yoga in menopause

In Western culture, menopause is the end of the menstrual cycle, a woman's fertile period. Because of this period's physical and emotional symptoms, the arrival of menopause is often associated with a decline in vitality.

In Eastern culture, the change in the body is not perceived negatively: it constitutes an opportunity to know oneself better and renew oneself.

Hormonal yoga follows this line of thinking, aiming not only at relaxation, like traditional hatha yoga but at stimulating vitality with exercises specific to hormone production.

By acting on the glands, hormone yoga therapy activates metabolism, improves circulation, and strengthens the immune system and the musculoskeletal system. These systems are the most affected by declining hormones, so hormone yoga is perfect for menopausal women's health.

# Here are the benefits you can get from hormonal yoga

### Reduction of menopausal symptoms

Signs such as hot flashes, night sweats, and headaches can be counteracted by stimulating the ovaries, helping your pre-menopause and after your last menstrual cycle.

### Regularization of sleep/wake rhythm and improvement of mood

The asana sequence that stimulates the glands promotes metabolism activation and brings balance back to the sleep/wake rhythm, warding off insomnia and daytime fatigue.

This also positively affects mood, reducing cortisol levels, fighting stress, and insomnia.

## Improved skin and hair health

Decreased ovarian function can make your skin and hair drier, so reactivating hormone production is a proper rejuvenation method. With constant practice, you can regain the beauty of your facial skin and feel younger.

## Rediscovery of libido

Hormonal imbalances and vaginal dryness can cause a drop in libido. Reactivating hormone production is an effective way to counteract this problem and regain sexual desire.

## Reducing the risks associated with hormonal decline

During menopause, the risk of osteoporosis and joint pain increases. You can counteract bone fragility with hormone yoga, strengthen your joints, and protect them by toning your muscles.

Remember to diet and exercise regularly, emphasize breathing, and clearly visualize your goals. By following these simple tips and a consistent method, you can decrease the disturbances that the natural decline of hormones poses for the musculoskeletal system.

# How to get started with yoga

## How Do You Get Started with Yoga?

If you have never practiced yoga, the best way to start is to rely on a qualified teacher. Even better if you share the practice of the discipline with a group of people. Yoga is a discipline suitable for everyone and perfect for any age: before starting, however, it is essential to point out to your teacher any medical conditions, from back pain to arthritis. The teacher will then be able to recommend the proper yoga postures that can benefit the whole body.

## How To Start Doing Yoga at Home On Your Own?

First of all, before you start practicing yoga on your own, it is best to take a few classes with a teacher: they will help you breathe the right way and perform the yoga postures correctly. Alternatively, you can turn to an "online" teacher to have guidance at the beginning of your journey before proceeding independently. One tip is to learn more about this ancient discipline by reading one or more books on the subject.

**To learn more:** To breathe well, you need to start with your nose. And learn how to use the diaphragm correctly.

## What Does It Take To Do Yoga?

To begin with, choose the home space in which to engage in yoga practice. There is no need for tools.

- Look for a room that is, if possible, empty but, most importantly, quiet

- If you prefer, furnish the room with scented candles, incense, or meditation cushions
- Wear comfortable clothing
- Purchase a yoga mat
- Consider doing yoga while listening, in the background, to music that can relax your body and mind
- Leave your phone in another room so that you are not disturbed by texts, emails, and phone calls

## What Style Of Yoga To Choose?

There is no set rule for choosing the type of yoga: experimenting with different styles will allow you to get closer to what your body needs most. However, hatha yoga is, in general, considered the manner with which to approach the discipline's practice.

## How Many Hours Of Yoga Per Day?

Generally, a class lasts, on average, an hour or so. However, workshops can last as long as 2 or 3 hours.

## How To Do Yoga Every Day

To get the full benefits, yoga must become a constant practice. It is not entirely essential to devote one or two hours a day to yoga; even half an hour can be enough.

The important thing is to carve out this half-hour every day. For example, a good habit might be to practice yoga early in the morning. This is also a great way to start the day with the right energy. Also, carve out a few minutes to devote to meditation. Gradually you will notice that it will become impossible to give up this healthy morning routine.

Also, consider inviting another friendly person to do yoga with you: sharing goals will help you be consistent and motivate each other.

# Yoga in pregnancy

Yoga can be a real panacea for expectant mothers because it simultaneously helps both body and spirit. As you move and smoothly stretch all your muscles, you are able. You become aware of your changing body, awakening its energy.

Here we explain why there is no reason to stop if you already practice yoga. On the contrary, pregnancy is the best time to start if you have never tried your hand at asana and pranayama.

The benefits of prenatal yoga have been the subject of several studies, such as one conducted by the Mayo Clinic, highlighting all the positive aspects of the discipline.

You can practice yoga in any trimester of pregnancy as long as you always listen to your body and its different needs without ever overdoing it. Here are the 10 good reasons to practice yoga during pregnancy.

## 1. Goodbye back pain

One of the most classic pregnancy complaints is back pain, as the spine is increasingly weighed down by the growing baby bump. In yoga, many stretching positions help posture and give immediate relief and relaxation in the lower back without any pain-relieving medication.

2. Relief in the first trimester with hormones in turmoil

The first trimester is a time of hormones in turmoil, nausea and fatigue, mood swings, and anxiety.

Every woman reacts differently to the onset of pregnancy; yoga can help you face this delicate and uncomfortable phase with serenity, but some precautions should be taken avoid jumping or extreme balancing positions that might bother the embryo, which is still settling.

## 3. Encourages contact with the baby

Yoga teaches us more about our bodies and offers many benefits for both mother and fetus. Through the different asanas and the moments of deep relaxation, the mother-to-be, typical of this discipline, learns to listen to herself and is thus able to get in touch with her baby in the belly soon as well.

## 4. Improves circulation

Through the regular exercise that this discipline offers, there is an improvement in blood and lymphatic circulation, which results in more minor swelling and heaviness in the legs.

## 5. Helps you sleep peaceful nights

Practicing yoga regularly also helps you sleep better. In addition to exercise, this discipline is also made up of a breathing part. Learning to practice deep, calm inhalations will activate the parasympathetic system, which helps regulate blood pressure and heart rate, aids digestion, and consequently, a good night's rest.

## 6. It is excellent preparation for childbirth

The various asanas practiced by the mother help the fetus gently find the correct position for birth inside the uterus. Meanwhile, the mother's pelvis gently and naturally expands in preparation for delivery. Incidentally, many yoga postures can prove to be comfortable positions for childbirth.

## 7. Teaches how to breathe

In yoga, one learns to breathe by inhaling and exhaling deeply through the nose, a beneficial technique for calming the mind in all stages of pregnancy. With practice, you focus on thoracic breathing, the so-called Ujjayi Breathing, which can prove to be a valuable technique for relieving the pains of childbirth naturally and, among other things, ensures a regular supply of oxygen to the baby.

## 8. Reduces anxiety and stress

When you are afraid of experiencing pain, your body produces adrenaline, which causes the bloodstream to simultaneously reduce oxytocin (the hormone that helps progress labor toward delivery). The practice of pranayama (yogic breathing) can calm the body and mind, reducing the factors that cause the body to produce adrenaline and helping expectant mothers during the difficult moments of childbirth.

### 9. Strengthens the body and gives energy

Regular yoga practice makes a mother-to-be's body stronger every day and ready to face all the hardships. Still, above all, the newly acquired inner strength will make the difference in coping with the new and challenging experience of parenthood.

## 10. Don't stop after childbirth

If practicing yoga brings so many benefits to mothers-to-be, it also gives just as many benefits to new mothers, so it is important not to stop when the baby is born. A few years ago, the University of Colorado showed that practicing yoga, especially breathing and meditation techniques, in the months after childbirth reduces the onset of postpartum depression. Prenatal yoga is a physical, bodily, and respiratory practice for pregnant women.

It helps to improve breathing and, for this reason, is most useful in pregnancy because better oxygenation of the maternal blood transmits more oxygen to the baby, thus promoting its optimal development.

In addition, it is also an excellent childbirth preparation course and teaches correct posture in daily life. By becoming more aware of your body, you feel more agile despite your belly and weight.

Prenatal yoga consists of simple movements and stretches that strengthen and stretch your muscles, which are highly stressed in the months leading up to childbirth.

During these yoga sessions, you learn to do many things:

- listen to your body and your emotions
- feel your baby and communicate with him
- relax
- Share your feelings with other moms
- accept the changes in your body
- Yoga and childbirth preparation
- Several postures help you work on opening your hips. These are exercises that help in preparation for childbirth.

During childbirth, breathing is essential. Pregnancy yoga teaches you the different breathing techniques to help you manage the strain and control the pain.

## To Avoid

During pregnancy, all inverted postures and some styles in particular such as Bikram yoga (yoga in the heat), which could lead to overheating of the body, are to be avoided.

Kapalabhati breathing - called "fire breathing" in Kundalini yoga - is also to be avoided, especially in the first trimester.

Interesting facts about yoga in pregnancy

Yoga during pregnancy is good for the mother, but it is also good for the baby. In fact, during its nine months in the mother's womb, the unborn baby absorbs the mother's moods and states of mind.

Practicing yoga helps one relax and get in touch with one's deep self. As a result, the feelings transmitted to the baby will be of harmony and inner peace, allowing to create balance in the unborn baby from the very first moments of its life.

## Are There Yoga Styles Contraindicated For Pregnant Women?

Several yoga centers have specialized in teaching breathing and relaxation techniques specifically for pregnant women in recent years. If you are already a practitioner, since yoga is a safe practice that follows your natural rhythms, you can also perform asana sequences from the comfort of your own home. It is always preferable to follow the instructions of a certified and experienced teacher, who will guide you in the necessary adjustments of the postures required during this period. Whether you decide to practice from home or choose to enroll in a class and be followed by a teacher, the most important thing is to listen to yourself and never strive beyond what your body suggests you do.

Currently, yoga centers offer different styles of yoga, some more physically demanding than others. The best choice when you are looking for a yoga class to practice during pregnancy is the specific prenatal yoga classes or the slower styles that emphasize breathing and mindfulness. If you decide to enroll in a course that is not specifically for pregnant women, always inform the teacher that you are pregnant before starting the class.

# How to do yoga at home

Have you recently started practicing in class and now would like to start doing yoga at home? Do you want to create your own practice safely and without hurting yourself?

The truth is that doing yoga at home is critically important for improving your practice. If you don't start practicing daily, it will take you much longer to see good results.

Going to class weekly is very important to understand how to do asanas correctly, build sequences, and know what mistakes to avoid so you don't hurt yourself. Still, it is even more important to start your practice at home.

This chapter will find why to do it, how best to start, turn your practice into a habit, and various video lessons to follow whenever and wherever you want.

When I started yoga, to tell you the truth, I never thought I would end up opening the mat every day. But initially, you are afraid of getting hurt, of performing the positions incorrectly. You don't know what kind of sequence to practice, so you do not do it.

In truth, these are just excuses that the mind throws at us. With time, however, we need to overcome these small fears, doubts, and insecurities and find a way to start

Here are the main reasons and benefits why you should do it:

Get to know yourself better

It is an only personal practice that allows you to feel your body, practice at your own pace, for as long as you wish, and relax into the asanas. Initially, it is not easy, but being self-taught allows you to develop a deep knowledge of yourself. This is precisely the basis that will enable you to improve your practice and life in general.

## For self-help

I, for one, started yoga for back pain, but others started for a wide variety of problems. Whatever your reason, if you limit yourself to only doing yoga in class occasionally, you will take much longer to feel better.

Practicing yoga at home is really helping yourself daily to improve your life and experience the profound benefits of yoga.

More significant improvements in less time

Practicing at home daily allows your body and mind to get used to everything you are doing much faster. The new yoga postures, recent efforts, and new difficulties you face.

When you practice every day, the effects of each session don't even have time to disappear, and therefore the improvements are incredible.

How to start correctly

It is essential to start doing yoga at home and equally crucial to do it correctly. Otherwise, you risk getting into the habit of doing the wrong practice and continuing to make the same mistakes for too long.

Here are some tips to make sure you practice correctly.

# Buy the professional mat

The mat is the first thing to buy when you start doing yoga. I say this because if you do not own one, it will happen you will have to use one that is in the studio

Check out the best mats in the shop and often, the ones that are made available for new practitioners are not the best; also, if you don't have one, you won't be able to practice at home but only in class, and this is certainly not the best way to get started. One last aspect to consider is that if the mat is not of good quality, indeed, as soon as you start to sweat, you will begin to slip. This does not allow you to practice at your best, but you might even hurt yourself. Better to avoid it, right?

So, my advice is to look for a quality one and make a minimum initial investment to get the best start, to be able to practice at home as well, and most importantly, to avoid injury.

# Take some classes

If you have never practiced yoga or have been practicing it for a short time anyway, the best thing to do is go to a class. Only a teacher can correct you, point you out if you make mistakes in alignments, advise you on the best asanas if you have a specific problem, show you how not to hurt yourself, and use supports to adjust the positions.

If you start totally self-taught, it might happen that you don't know that you are making inevitable mistakes. Therefore, you keep making them for a long time. Better to avoid that, right?

My advice is to go a minimum of a couple of times a week to class so you can put the foundation for proper practice, and for the rest, practice at home whenever you can.

# Choose the correct type of yoga for you

There are so many types of yoga that can be practiced now, and when you start out, there is some confusion about which one to choose. This is because there are really all kinds, from the more static to the more eventful, from the more meditative to the more physical, and from the more modern to the more traditional.

Choosing the right one, depending on what you are like and what kind of life you are leading, is most important because only then will you experience more benefits from the practice.

On the contrary, if you are practicing a style that is too slow for you or too dynamic, you may give up the practice. It is really a great pity if you do this only because you have not found the right style.

My advice is to try more than one until you feel that type of practice is suitable for the way you are and continue that type of practice.

## Make it a perfect habit

Suppose you have only recently started doing yoga. When you begin your practice at home, you will realize that it is not that easy, and you will undoubtedly feel slightly disoriented.

But don't worry, it's something you're doing for the first time and, as with all new things, it's normal for it to take time to become familiar.

Follow the following tips, and I am sure they will enable you to start and continue your practice at home in the best way possible. It becomes a beautiful habit that you will never be able to give up. MMA

## Start gradually

There is absolutely no point in starting the practice by doing two hours a day every day. The body is not used to it, and neither is the mind. In this way, you will overstep your limits at that time, and that is not good. You may feel exhausted or, even worse, you may get injured.

So, my advice is to start moderately, perhaps with 20 minutes a day, and then gradually increase over time both the length of practice and the difficulty of the positions.

## Choose the right kind of practice

The beauty of practicing has a home where you can decide how you want to practice at your leisure. First, however, it is most important to listen to your body and identify what it needs at that moment. I consider this to be one of the most critical aspects of practice because only by listening carefully to the signals it sends you will you have a method that allows you to feel better.

- If you ignore what the body is communicating to you, not only are you not doing yoga, but you may be hurting yourself.

- Here are some examples of adapting the practice according to your situation.

- If you have a job where you sit all day, you might do a practice consisting mainly of standing yoga postures to strengthen your legs.
- Conversely, if you walk all day at work, you could do mainly floor poses and asanas to relax your body and legs.
- If you have back pain, you could do a practice to make the pain affecting the spine disappear.

If you practice in the morning, you could do a more invigorating type of practice. Still, a more relaxing approach is definitely better if you practice in the evening.

If you have neck pain, you could do yoga to relax the entire neck area.

These are examples to show you how you can very well adapt the practice at home depending on how you feel at the time. Of course, it takes some time to learn to listen to the body and modify the method according to different situations, but it will all come with time.

## Being realistic

Another aspect to consider making the practice a good habit is to be realistic with yourself. Being natural means considering many factors such as your age, how tired you are at that moment, your flexibility, how much time you have, etc. Only if you are will you be able to do an adequate and, above all, beneficial practice.

There is no point in trying to be able to do challenging postures if you are a few years older or have a physical problem. Instead, try to do the simpler asanas well.

Same thing if you are not too flexible, it doesn't matter. Yoga is not about being flexible. Try to push your personal limits, but don't try to get to do asanas that require extreme flexibility. Otherwise, you will only hurt yourself.

## Add the practice into your daily schedule.

To make yoga significantly improve your life, the first thing you need to do is to do it daily. So, try to add it among the many items you have to do every day. Especially the first few times you practice, yoga should be a "commitment" to be carried out with sacrifice.

I specified "especially the first few times" because the greatest sacrifice happens the first few times you do the exercises. Once you begin to experience the many benefits, much easier to give up other, less important things so that yoga has more space in your life.

Find your sacred space at home.

One more piece of advice I can give you to make yoga at home an excellent routine is to find your own "sacred space" to enter each time you practice.

This sacred space could be a small room, a garage, a garden, or simply your mat.

It does not matter how big it is or where it is located.

The important thing is that when you go into it, you leave everything not related to your yoga practice out of this space. Leave out your cell phone, daily problems, hurry, ego, worries, and anything else that can distract you from the practice. You can resume it as soon as you are finished with your exercises.

# Pranayama

Life begins with an inhale and ends with an exhale. It is a fact, a universal law that makes no distinction of sex, age, or skin color.

And it is precisely the belief that our breaths are somehow counted and that the fewer we take, the longer we live that gave rise to the breathing techniques known as Pranayama.

According to one of the most authoritative Hatha Yoga texts, Patanjali's Yoga Sutras, Pranayama constitutes one of the eight Angas, or stages or **"limbs"** of yoga.

Actually, by the term Pranayama we do not only mean the breathing techniques used by yoga, but the mechanism by which prana, or life energy, can be absorbed and controlled to make the mind stable, strong, peaceful, and being able to awaken its latent potentialities. (Which we often do not even imagine we possess.)

"Prana, in fact, means energy, or vital breath that fills the universe."

According to a mystical view, the vital energy flows within every being and thus represents our source of sustenance.

The primary source of prana is the air we breathe. Still, in reality, we also absorb it from food and drink, which is why in yoga, great importance is attached to nose and tongue hygiene, slow chewing, and, of course, effective breathing.

In fact, prana is absorbed through the mucous membranes of the nose and by the nerve receptors of the respiratory system, but also through the nerve endings of the tongue and throat.

On the other hand, the word Ayama means "extension" or "expansion"; therefore, the word Pranayama means "extension or expansion of the size of prana."

That is a method of absorbing and directing life energy in the body, making the mind stable and reaching a higher level of consciousness.

Also, according to Patanjali's Yoga Sutras, the step preceding Pranayama is the practice of asanas, that is, postures, which have the primary purpose of making the body agile, flexible, and relaxed, freeing it from nervous movements and muscle tension.

When the body is "under control," it is easy to turn our attention to the breath, which acts as a conduit between the materiality of the body and the spirituality of the mind, and this allows us, through Pranayama, to achieve the union of these two elements, and then move on to the next step, which is profound meditation, through the retraction of the senses. Pranayama is also a valuable method for preventing and curing many ailments...however, the effectiveness of Pranayama as prevention is more significant than its therapeutic effectiveness.

The benefits of Pranayama are, in fact, numerous:

- It facilitates the elimination of toxins.
- Improves blood and lymphatic circulation.
- It optimizes the filtering action of the kidneys.
- Tones the nervous system.
- Acts positively on memory.
- Aids digestion.
- Frees from negative thoughts and fears that immobilize intent.

- Purifies the nadis. (The energy channels of the body).

- Stimulates the spleen.

- Balances the glandular system.

- Strengthens the immune system.

## Why does Pranayama work?

Numerous experiments show that vital functions are minimized during pranayama practice, such as the heart pumping blood more slowly and resting (except in some methods such as kapalabhati). In addition, the mind relaxes as it is subject to less workload.

If the body is relaxed, the mind does not need to expend energy to send contraction impulses to the muscles, and what ensues is a state of mental peace.

Pranayama improves respiratory function by exercising the breathing muscles and influencing the respiratory centers. Hence, one gains the ability to breathe more efficiently.

Pranayama works because during practice we make full use of our lung capacity, thus improving the oxygenation of the whole body for the benefit of every cell.

The organs receive oxygen and receive plenty of blood, and their efficiency is increased.

Pressure changes in the rib cage are intensified, which means better blood circulation between one cavity and another. When the pressure difference is significant, circulation increases.

Pressure changes stress the compressed and decompressed organs by improving their functions.

With some training in pranayama practice, one can experience peace of mind, reduction of tension, increased sense of well-being, order, and discipline in one's behavior.

Therefore, the practice of pranayama techniques can potentially improve every aspect of our personality.

## How does one breathe in Pranayama?

Breathing is a natural process that accompanies us throughout our existence:

- Through the inhale, we assimilate oxygen necessary for maintaining the body.

- Through exhalation, we eliminate toxins harmful to the body, such as carbon dioxide.

Unlike other involuntary processes, such as digestion, breathing is a spontaneous act with which we can somehow interact; in fact, we can decide to breathe more or less profoundly or even stop breathing for a short time.

This happens because there are nerve centers that regulate the respiratory activity, sending the impulse that allows inhalation and exhalation. On the other hand, through other brain impulses, we can partially inhibit involuntary processes and thus decide how to breathe.

During pranayama practice, all the muscles in the body are relaxed, which helps put the body and mind in a state of complete rest, eliminates mental tension, and significantly influences physiological functions.

The exciting thing is that anyone can practice pranayama techniques. There is no physical or age limitation that prevents it.

Suppose you can't wait to start learning how to breathe correctly. In that case, I suggest you start with the first step toward proper Pranayama, searching for breath uniformity.

## Before you approach actual Pranayama, your breath must be uniform.

This is an easy goal to achieve and costs very little in terms of time; you just need to equip yourself with a stopwatch and a few minutes to devote to your breath. (I explain how to do this below).

Usually, pranayama exercises are done while sitting in a meditative position; unfortunately, for many people, it is challenging to be able to maintain this position without experiencing discomfort or pain, thus compromising the success of the practice.

Therefore, if you find it uncomfortable to get into a meditative position, you can sit cross-legged, perhaps using a block or book to put under your butt to help you keep your back straight without experiencing discomfort or pain during the practice, or you can use pillows to put under your knees.

Or you can also place yourself in a chair with the soles of your feet resting on the floor.

An important factor in successful practice is maintaining a comfortable, stable, and relaxed posture.

Your back must be straight, your head in line with your spine, your shoulders, and your neck wholly simple.

## Ready? Let's get started

1.  Relax your hands on your knees.
2.  Relax your shoulders and neck.
3.  Begin to listen to your breath by remaining attentive to the air entering and leaving your nostrils.
4.  Do not try to modify the breath but simply listen.

When the breath has relaxed, start the stopwatch and measure how long it takes you to take 10 slow, deep breaths.

Write down the duration of the 10 breathing cycles. (This usually varies from 2 to 5 minutes, but it is subjective.)

When you can finish the breathing cycles in the same amount of time, you will have reached the first level of Pranayama, which is breath uniformity.

It may take a few days or months, which is also subjective.

Most people approach pranayama techniques without achieving breath uniformity; obviously, this is no big deal. It was like that for me, and I am still alive. Still, it is equally evident that the practice will be more efficient if we approach Pranayama with the proper preparation. Then, we can enjoy all its benefits to the fullest.

Haven't you been dying to wake up in the morning and time your breaths?

Well, now you have a good reason to do it!!!

# Yoga and nutrition

Healthy and balanced nutrition is a vital component of a holistic practice such as yoga. Even non-practitioners know that it is not the physical activity for its own sake: yoga is a way of life that, as such, involves all spheres of existence, including nutrition. And if you are a yogi, you know that yoga practitioners often follow a vegetarian or vegan diet. What we eat, in fact, (self-)defines us. Each must be consistent with their own values and morals. However, this article will not address the exciting concept of ethical eating: we will just give you some pointers on good food for those who practice yoga consistently, with a suitable energy supply to the muscles involved in the exercises.

## The importance of quantities

Before we point you to what foods are suitable for yogis, let's focus on quantities to be kept in check. Let's face it, this should be done in general, not just if you practice yoga. Dosing the amounts of food introduced into our bodies is a good sign of balance, which never hurts. Being more "concrete" matters. If you overeat, you risk feeling bloated and irritable. If you eat too little, your muscles do not have enough strength to cope with the practice.

Remember that the more muscles are exercised, the more they consume it's a simple "rule" of our body that we often forget about, even though it's fundamental to rethinking our approach to food.

You may be wondering, yes, but how much should I eat? You don't have to think in terms of grams or calories. You simply have to listen to your body and understand when to take in food. Instead, you need to limit yourself. Listen to yourself, just as you do when you practice yoga.

## Eat following the body's natural rhythm.

Speaking of yoga, as we also remarked above, you cannot ignore the concept of balance. To achieve it, we recommend that you eat at regular times and intervals, in line with your body's natural rhythm.

## Foods beneficial for the body and mind

Not all foods are suitable for yoga practitioners. They mustn't be loaded with sugars and substances that are difficult to digest, which are likely to make you hungover. Instead, it is better to choose foods high in energy and low in calories, such as fruits, vegetables, and legumes.

According to Ayurveda, what we eat also influences our emotions and thoughts because each food is considered for its effects on the body and mind. According to Ayurvedic nutrition, some foods purify the body and calm the mind. Others lead to action, and others urge inertia. One should favor the former, not overdo the latter, and avoid the latter.

It is interesting to note that the foods considered healthiest for the ancient masters of Ayurveda are also the same for proponents of the Mediterranean diet. In detail, it is vital to have a balanced diet with the right amount of nutrients to practice yoga: so, make way for fiber, vitamins, natural sugars, and healthy fats.

## The ideal foods for yoga practice

And so here we come to the foods that help purify the body and mind: fresh fruit, green leafy vegetables, grains, and dried fruits (among which we recall nuts), as well as some spices and roots. Ginger, for example, fresh or powdered, is considered an integral part of the diet for its digestive and decongestant properties. At the same time, turmeric is an excellent remedy for muscle aches.

To be avoided are fried foods and foods with a long shelf life, excessively fatty (especially saturated fats, the most harmful), and those high in sugar.

A balanced daily diet, therefore, includes fiber and protein. When combined with grains, the latter contributes to the formation of noble amino acids, readily assimilated by the body and muscle tissue. In addition, remember that legumes, particularly lentils, are rich in iron, which can be better absorbed if you consume foods such as citrus fruits, which are rich in vitamin C, which promotes its assimilation.

Suppose you don't follow a vegetarian or vegan diet. In that case, we recommend taking fish (especially anchovies, cod, salmon, tuna, mackerel, and other types of oily fish), which, thanks to Omega 3, helps fight muscle inflammation and reduce lactic acid after physical exertion. As well as aiding cardiovascular circulation.

Still, it should be the first good rule to give and follow when it comes to healthy eating: remember to hydrate yourself consistently, drinking at least 11 cups a day, including in the form of herbal teas and infusions.

## What foods to take?

Those who practice yoga and assimilate it into their lifestyle generally prefer a vegetarian or vegan diet, in line with moral maxims such as nonviolence, which applies to all living beings. According to these values, what we eat also defines us: our diet must be consistent with our values and ethics. Unfortunately, however, not everyone manages to be so adherent to this way of life, especially those who are just getting into the practice.

In any case, universal foods can still be established for anyone who wants to strengthen their muscular system, support toning, and gain energy.

A curious finding: by reviewing the favored items, we can see that the healthiest foods for the ancient masters of Ayurveda are also fit for devotees of the Mediterranean diet. In particular, it is essential to have a balanced diet with the right amount of nutrients for the body and for practicing yoga: so, go for fiber, vitamins, natural sugars, and healthy fats.

Returning to the foods that help purify the body and mind: these are fresh fruits, green leafy vegetables, grains, milk, and nuts (especially almonds), as well as some spices and roots. For example, both fresh and powdered ginger is considered an indispensable part of the diet because of their digestive and decongestant properties.

The foods that stimulate us and should be taken in limited quantities are spicy foods, onions, garlic, tea, coffee, and fried foods. Conversely, among those that would be best avoided, we find foods with a long shelf life, excessively fatty (especially saturated fats, which are the most harmful), and those high in sugar.

A balanced daily diet should be rich in fiber and protein to aid in yoga practice. The latter can come from fish and legumes. When combined with grains, they form a winning combination thanks to creating noble amino acids readily assimilated by the body and muscle tissues.

Legumes, particularly lentils, are rich in iron, which can be better absorbed if foods such as citrus fruits are taken, which have always been carriers of vitamin C, which precisely promotes its assimilation.

Those who cannot follow a vegetarian or vegan diet can fall back on fish (especially anchovies, cod, Atlantic salmon, tuna, mackerel, and other types of oily fish), which, thanks to Omega 3, helps fight muscle inflammation (even trivially reduce lactic acid after physical exertion) and promotes cardiovascular circulation.

Never forget to keep yourself well hydrated: drinking at least two liters of water a day, including in the form of herbal teas and infusions.

# Yoga Poses

Basic Asanas are the Yoga Positions most commonly used in dynamic practices, warm-ups, or transitional Asanas.

Practiced with the correct alignments, they are basic exercises that stabilize and strengthen the spine.

## The Mountain (TADASANA)

Between Heaven and Earth, from the roots of the 1st Chakra, Muladhara, to the Spirituality of Sahasrara, the Crown Chakra.

In the stability of the feet, with the force of the Inhale, the top of the head pushes toward Heaven.

The spine relaxes. Posture improves.

Tadasana increases body awareness and tones the abdominals and buttocks. It also strengthens the legs by correcting flat feet and bad knees.

Practiced regularly, it improves stability and balance.

Standing still as a mountain is a challenge to stand still in mind, stopping the whirlwind of thoughts.

## Dogface Down Position (ADHO MUKHA SVANASANA)

Among the Hatha Yoga Positions, the most popular, Adho Mukha Svanasana, fully stretches the spine, relieving back pain when practiced correctly.

It stretches the muscles of the back of the body. In addition, it strengthens the shoulders and arms by loosening any stiffness in the shoulder blades.

On an energetic level, it mainly stimulates the energies of the Chakras, Muladhara, and Svadhisthana, while giving a burst of power to the whole body. It relieves fatigue and physical stress and relaxes the mind.

To enter asana correctly and comfortably, the exhalation is of great help. It pushes the abdomen toward the legs and of the coccyx upward.

# Cat Position (MARJARIASANA)

Quadrupedal position with remarkable benefits. Often practiced in warm-ups alternating with Bitilasana, the Cow of India.

Makes the spine flexible while massaging the internal organs.

Relieves lower back pain and tension by strengthening the abdominals. Excellent to practice during the menstrual period to alleviate pain and regulate the cycle.

Marjariasana stimulates the nervous system by improving balance and concentration.

The alternating movement of the pelvis is coordinated with the breath, starting with the inhale. It mainly moves the energies of the 2nd Chakra Svadhisthana.

Standing Yoga Positions

Standing Yoga Asanas, Partial Balance Positions, are very energizing, stimulate concentration and promote action.

# Standing Yoga Positions

Standing Yoga Asanas, Partial Balance Positions, are very energizing, stimulate concentration and promote action.

## First Warrior Position (VIRABHADRASANA I)

Stability in the feet, firmness in the pelvis, and opening of the chest encourage the energies of Muladhara, Svadhisthana, and Anahata Chakra.

Virabhadrasana, I corrects posture and improves breathing by opening the chest; strengthens and lengthens leg and back muscles, providing relief in cases of sciatica; stretches and relaxes the psoas.

Warming, stimulating, and energizing Yoga asana; prevents and relieves digestive problems.

The posture brings us back to the image of Shiva inhaling, stretching toward the sky, and pointing his sword.

## Second Warrior Position (VIRABHADRASANA II)

With feet firmly on the earth, Inhaling, Shiva points his sword at the enemy.

Virabhadrasana II mainly stimulates the energies of Muladhara and Svadhisthana.

It strengthens and lengthens the muscles of the body. In addition, it stretches the hip flexors and tones the abdomen and internal organs.

It stimulates the thyroid and parathyroid glands and is valuable therapeutic aid for sciatica, carpal tunnel syndrome, and infertility.

# Third Warrior Position (VIRABHADRASANA III)

Balancing posture, it is the lightness of Inhale instability.

Virabhadrasana III strengthens the neck, back muscles, abdominals, legs, and ankles.

It gives flexibility and agility. Improves cardiovascular function.

The grounding of the foot in support invokes the energies of the earth.

Stimulates Muladhara and Svadhistana. Abdominal strength, needed to support the lengthening torso, boosts Manipura Chakra energy.

## The Extended Triangle Pose (UTTHITA TRIKONASANA)

Trikonasana, the Triangle Position, takes us back to the religious concept of the Hindu Trimurti, Brahma, Vishnu, and Shiva.

So also like the philosophical concepts that identify the three primordial forces of nature in Sattva, Rajas, and Tamas.

For proper execution of Asana Yoga, it is good to stretch the body forward by inhaling. Then flex the torso sideways, Exhaling.

Trikonasana moves the energies of Muladhara and Svadhisthana. It is a Polar Position since it acts on the Yin, the female, and Yang, the male poles.

The Triangle Position strengthens the pelvic organs and tones the abdominals. In addition, it improves peristaltic bowel movements, stretches the adductors, and extends the spine, chest, arms, shoulders, and neck.

It also strengthens the back muscles of the body, ankles, and knees, increasing physical endurance.

## The Extended Hip Yoga Position (UTTHITA PARSVAKONASANA)

Excellent Hatha Yoga Lunging Position for stretching the hip flexors and strengthening the muscles of the legs and ankles.

Expanding the chest improves breathing capabilities, also benefiting the circulatory and digestive systems.

Parsvakonasana strengthens the abdominals and upper body muscles, front and back, stretches the spine, and strengthens the back.

Like all Standing Positions, it mainly stimulates the energies of Muladhara and Svadhisthana Chakra but also Manipura. It is a downward flexion that requires an Exhale to correctly enter Asana.

## The Strength Posture (UTKATASANA)

Commonly known as the Chair Position, it resumes the act of sitting in an Espiro, relying only on the muscle power of the legs.

It is a very energizing Yoga Position that stimulates Manipura and Anahata Chakra in the stability of Muladhara earth energies.

Utkatasana strengthens the ankles, calves, and generally the legs. In addition, it reduces the flat foot and stretches the Achilles tendon.

Stretches and strengthens the muscles of the spine, improving related disorders.

Tones the lower abdomen, Improves breathing, diaphragm excursions, and heart contractions.

Standing Balance Yoga Positions

Standing Balance Yoga Positions represent the ability to live "What is" in the present moment.

A physical balance that reflects the balance of a serene and stable mind.

## The Tree Posture (VRKSASANA)

The best known and most practiced Yoga Position. Steadfast as trees sinking their roots into the earth. Nourish the energies of the 1st and 2nd Chakras, Muladhara and Swadhisthana until the branches extend to the sky in the Inhale.

Vrksasana improves balance and serenades the mind while also stimulating Ajna Chakra.

It strengthens thighs, ankles, and calves by reducing flat feet.

It relaxes the spine, relieving related issues such as tension, lower back pain, and sciatica.

## The Garuda Yoga Posture (GARUDASANA)

More commonly known as the Eagle Yoga Posture.

Garudasana requires excellent concentration in its execution, on par with the sharpness of an eagle.

The stability of balance in the Inhale and all the energy of Svadhisthana and Ajna Chakra in holding it.

Garudasana improves the ability to stay in balance, physical and mental. It strengthens the hips and ankles. Stretches the calves, thighs, and hips and stretches the back area.

## The Yoga Posture of the Half Moon (ARDHA CHANDRASANA)

Laughs the Moon at the ruinous fall of Ganesha, who, with all his wrath, strikes her with his fang.

Ardha Chandrasana, in its posture, recalls the moment when Ganesha, with an Inhale, soars upward to strike the Moon.

It is a Position of balance and grounding that primarily stimulates Muladhara and Svadhisthana Chakra.

It improves balance, stability, and strength in the grace and elegance of a Yoga Asana.

It strengthens the ankles, leg muscles, knees, and buttocks on a physical level. In addition, it improves hip mobility and strengthens and stretches the spine.

Among other benefits, it improves digestion by relieving gastric disorders.

## The Yoga Position of the Extended Hand to the Big Toe (UTTHITA HASTA PADANGUSTASANA)

Hatha Yoga pose of balance is not the easiest to maintain. A real challenge is to remain calm in mind in support of the Inhale.

Utthita Hasta Padangustasana mainly stimulates the gross energies of the Muladhara and Svadhisthana Chakras.

It strengthens the ankles and leg muscles by lengthening the posterior chains. Improves physical balance and calms the mind.

# Yoga Positions with Back Extension

Open with joy to the world around you by stimulating the energy of Anahata, the Heart Chakra. Elevate the human component above the more instinctive one.

## The Yoga Position of the Cobra (BHUJANGASANA)

Awareness grows in Silence, like a Cobra that moves sinuously without making a sound in the Inhale.

The extension and expansion of the chest in the Bhujangasana Position primarily move the energies of Anahata and Vishudda Chakra.

It is a Yoga Position that provides significant physical and mental benefits.

It strengthens the wrists, arms, shoulders, and back. In addition, it makes the spine flexible, improves posture, and relieves lower back pain and sciatica.

Expands the chest by facilitating breathing, respiratory ailments, and asthma.

Tones the abdomen and internal organs, especially the pancreas and adrenal glands.

Effective in relieving pain and menstrual irregularities. Stimulates Agni while also improving digestion and constipation. Reduces intestinal gas. Excellent position in mild depressive disorders. Relieves stress and fatigue.

## The Yoga Position of the Bow (DHANURASANA)

Dhanurasana acts as a natural massage on the internal organs.

At the abdominal level, it helps reduce excess fat. In addition, it relieves menstrual pain and revitalizes the genital system.

Reduces gastrointestinal disorders and aids digestion.

Backward extension of the torso lengthens and makes the spine flexible by toning the spinal nerves.

Chest expansion improves breathing, diaphragm mobility, and respiratory system affections.

Dhanurasana improves the function of the cardiovascular system. In addition, it strengthens the back muscles and lengthens those in the front part of the body.

On an energetic level, it mainly stimulates the energies of the Chakras, Manipura, and Anahata. The impetus in lifting the upper body is in the Inhale.

## Royal Pigeon Yoga Position on One Leg (EKA PADA RAJAKAPOTASANA)

Hatha Yoga posture is among the most beautiful to look at but not the easiest to practice.

Eka Pada Rajakapotasana requires perseverance, patience, preparation, and profound Inhale ability.

The expansion of the chest and stretching of the entire front part of the body improves the respiratory and cardiac abilities and the elasticity of the diaphragm.

It is a very energizing Position. It stimulates the thyroid and adrenal glands and helps with mild depressive disorders.

It makes the spine, hips, and shoulders flexible at the physical level.

At the energetic level, it moves the energies of the Anahata and Vishudda Chakras.

## The Yoga Posture of "Hanuman" (HANUMANASANA)

Hanumanasana takes us back to Hindu mythology. Hanuman is the Lord of the monkeys who can fly.

The Yoga Posture, more commonly known as sagittal split, is precisely reminiscent of him flying with the full force of the Inhale.

It is an advanced Asana that requires commitment and perseverance but has remarkable benefits.

It relaxes and tones the leg muscles. In addition, it intensely stretches the posterior tendons of the front leg.

It simultaneously stretches the psoas and flexors of the back leg. Strengthens and makes the hip joint elastic. Stimulates the abdominal organs. Valuable therapeutic aid in cases of sciatica. At the energetic level, it works mainly on Svadhisthana and Anahata Chakra.

## The Yoga Position of the Fish (MATSYASANA)

Matsyasana, the Fish Posture, is not the easiest to perform. It requires a large opening of the chest.

But with a bit of patience and a lot of perseverance, it will be possible to start practicing it in the most superficial variations, for example, by bringing yourself into elbow support.

Excellent yoga asana for improving posture. It makes the back area of the back and the whole spine flexible. Stretches the front part of the body, abdominals, pectorals and neck, hip flexors, and intercostal muscles.

It relieves menstrual pain and benefits constipation. In addition, opening the chest improves breathing and benefits the cardiovascular system.

It is a very energizing Yoga Position that mainly stimulates Manipura, Anahata, and Vishudda.

Beneficial in cases of anxiety and mild depression.

## The Yoga Position of the Locust (SALABHASANA)

Salabhasana is an invitation to live with gusto in the present moment. Like a locust taking great leaps forward with courage, heedless of the past.

In the force of the Inhale, the torso and legs rise up, releasing and stimulating the energies of Manipura and Anahata.

It is an activating and energizing Yoga Position, therefore excellent in cases of stress and mild depressive problems.

It strengthens the spine's muscles, making it elastic and preventing lower back pain. Stretches the rib cage improving respiratory problems such as asthma. Strengthens and lengthens leg muscles and abdominal muscles. Relieves flatulence, constipation, and indigestion.

# The Contracted Bridge Yoga Position (SETU BANDHA SARVANGASANA)

The pelvis pushes upward in the force of the Inhale in a Hatha Yoga posture with multiple benefits.

It makes the spine elastic and tones the abdomen and pelvic area. Stretches and strengthens all the muscles of the body. Stimulates the thyroid, lungs, and abdominal organs.

Chest expansion improves breathing and is helpful in cases of asthma, high blood pressure, osteoporosis, and sinusitis.

Setu Bandha Sarvangasana is a relaxing yet energizing asana. It reduces anxiety, fatigue, headaches, and insomnia.

It gives vigor to tired legs and relieves back pain.

It works mainly on the Anahata and Vishudda Chakras on an energetic level.

# The Yoga Position of the Lying Hero (SUPTA VIRASANA)

Supta Virasana is a Hatha Yoga posture to be performed with caution and proper preparation. Alternatively, it can be practiced using a support under the back.

Essential to enter Asana progressively. Recline back slowly during the Exhale.

Then Inhale while expanding the chest.

Notables are its benefits: it stretches and stretches quadriceps, abdominals, and psoas. But, on the other hand, it hurts and relaxes the pelvic area.

It stretches the hips, knees, and lower back. Reduces fatigue and heaviness in the legs, purifying them of lactic acid. Reduces the tendency to varicose veins and edema in the lower limbs.

Stimulates liver and intestines by improving digestive functions and stomach disorders. A valuable antidote to nausea even during the pregnancy period.

It is a relaxing posture that calms the mind and energetically stimulates Svadhisthana and Anahata energies.

## The Yoga Position of the Bow (URDHVA DHANURASANA)

Very intense Hatha Yoga posture. Also known as Chakrasana for its ability to engage all the Chakras. Although, since it is a solemn opening of the chest, it works primarily on Anahata.

The force of a deep Inhale along with well-grounded feet and hands is required for the upward thrust.

Urdhva Dhanurasana strengthens the legs and buttocks. Elasticizes the spine and back region. Intensively extends the entire front part of the body. Tones pelvic organs and abdomen. Strengthens arms and wrists. Improves breathing and makes the body agile.

Energizing and vitalizing Asana is a valuable aid in cases of mild depression. Has a stimulating effect on the nervous and endocrine systems?

## The Face-Up Dog Yoga Position (URDHVA MUKHA SVANASANA)

Energizing Yoga posture is characterized by extending the spine and opening the chest. Expansion in the Inhale progressively improves breathing skills.

Very useful for eliminating back stiffness and enhancing muscle tone by alleviating low back pain and sciatica.

Improves and corrects posture and gait. Stretches and lengthens the front part of the body. It tones the buttocks and activates Agni, the digestive fire, stimulating metabolism.

It nourishes Manipura, Anahata, and Vishudda Chakra on an energetic level. Very effective in mild depressive disorders.

## Camel Yoga Position (USTRASANA)

Very intense Hatha Yoga posture. It is to be practiced after adequate preparation, a good warm-up, and a deep Inhale.

Ustrasana is an opening with a backward extension. It deeply stretches the front part of the body, thighs, ankles, and groin.

It strengthens the buttocks, arms, and shoulders. Strengthens back muscles by making the back area elastic. Stretches the hip flexors.

Very energizing position, helpful in mild depression, and mainly stimulates Anahata and Vishudda Chakra.

Inversion Yoga Positions.

Transcend one's fears and be open to the Sacredness of the Discipline.

Changing energy polarities to reverse mental patterns and make up for lack of imagination.

## The Yoga Posture of the Upside-Down Tree (ADHO MUKHA VRKSASANA)

More commonly known as the handstand, Adho Mukha Vrksasana is a very energizing Yoga Position.

It often frightens novices but can be practiced safely by preparing the body gradually.

The strength of the Inhale and the activation of the abdominals in the energy of Manipura are valuable to aid in pushing upward.

It is a Position that strengthens the shoulders, arms, wrists, and back. It also increases the rib cage volume, bringing significant benefits to breathing.

A very energizing asana, it activates and revitalizes the body. Improves blood circulation and metabolism.

## The Yoga Position of the Plow (HALASANA)

Yoga posture with powerful symbolism.

The feet beyond the head are like the wedge that turns the earth. The search for one's inner potential is necessary for evolution.

Asana with remarkable physical and mental benefits.

Relaxes and stretches the spine while improving posture. Performs a therapeutic function for back pain. Tones the internal organs of the abdomen. Drains liver and pancreas, improving digestive and intestinal problems.

Stimulates the pelvic area and circulation at the pelvic level and blood circulation in general. Relieves and reduces stress and fatigue. Relaxes the mind.

It is an excellent therapeutic position for asthma. It refreshes the body by stimulating mainly Vishudda Chakra. Since this is a backward bend, it is important to scout the abdomen and chest with a full Exhale to correctly enter the Asana.

## The Yoga Position of the Royal Peacock (PINCHA MAYURASANA)

Hatha Yoga poses resting on the forearms exceptionally energizing and revitalizing. Promotes venous return to the heart. Improves circulation and mainly stimulates Manipura and Anahata.

Being able to practice Pincha Mayurasana is a great challenge. It enables one to gain more self-confidence by improving physical and mental balance.

It tones all the internal organs. It strengthens the muscles of the shoulders, arms, and back. It increases the expansion of the chest.

To enter the Asana correctly, the Inhale is essential.

## Candle Yoga Position (SALAMBA SARVANGASANA)

The Yoga Position of the Upright Trunk. Commonly known as the candle, it is a valuable aid in regulating blood pressure and improving thyroid function. It mainly stimulates the energies of the Vishudda Chakra.

Among other benefits, it strengthens shoulders and arms. In addition, it stimulates the internal abdominal organs and digestion, pelvic organs, and prostate.

It makes the spine elastic. Therapeutic yoga asana for asthma and sinusitis.

Refreshing and rejuvenating relieves stress, fatigue, and symptoms of insomnia. Valuable aid in cases of mild depression.

The upward push of the body requires the Inhale to bring oneself comfortably into the position.

## Yoga Position on the Head (SIRSHASANA)

Among the Positions, it is perhaps the most sought after by newbies, eager to maintain balance on the elbows and top of the head.

Sirsasana opens to the Spirituality of Yoga, mainly stimulating the Crown Chakra, Sahasrara.

Beautiful to practice and watch, it requires Inhaling to correctly enter the position and enjoy the public benefits extended to the whole body.

Valuable Yoga asana reduces the body's load on the lumbar vertebrae and realigns the spine. In addition, strengthens the arms, shoulders, neck, and trunk muscles.

Facilitates venous return from lower limbs and pelvis improving circulation and disorders such as varicose veins and hemorrhoids, prolapses, and water retention.

Decongests the genitals and liver. Regulates blood pressure and improves digestion. Stimulating the pituitary gland and endocrine system regulates metabolism and helps intellectual functions: attention, concentration, and memory.

Sirsasana increases self-confidence and optimism.

## Yoga Positions of Strength

Strength Asanas are those Yoga Positions that predominantly engage Manipura, the 3rd Chakra. They stimulate the power of affirmation and self-esteem. They increase the ability to remain stable in the face of life's obstacles.

# The Yoga Posture of the Crow (BAKASANA)

Whether Bakasana or Kakasana, Crane Position or Crow Position, it matters little since they differ only in the alignment of the arms.

An asana of strength but also of balance, it develops patience and concentration in the precision of an Inhale and the power of Manipura. Bakasana strengthens shoulders, arms, pectorals, and wrists. It activates the abdominals and adductors. Strengthens and opens the groin.

## The Grounded Stick Yoga Position (CHATURANGA DANDASANA)

Also known as the Leaning Position on the four "anga" or limbs, this is a very intense Yoga Asana and not the easiest to maintain.

Exhaling achieved it, but it takes a good deal of strength to keep the body on one line, power stimulated by the Manipura Chakra focus.

Chaturanga Dandasana strengthens the arms by developing the triceps. It supports the wrists, shoulders, and back muscles. Improves body awareness and posture. Strengthens the abdomen and, in a general way, the whole body.

## The Boat Yoga Posture (NAVASANA)

Yoga asana of strength but also of balance on the ischia. It is so-called because it brings back the shape of a rowboat.

Navasana primarily stimulates and tones the abdominal muscles while strengthening the muscles that support the spine and hip flexors. It improves the functioning of the kidneys, thyroid, prostate, and intestines. Stimulates the Fire Chakra, Manipura. Improves metabolism by strengthening self-esteem.

Energizing posture requires the Inhale in its correct entry.

## The Yoga Position of "Vasistha." (VASISTHASANA)

Translated by some as a side bench, Vasisthasana is actually the Yoga Position of the sage Vasistha. The first of Brahma's mind-born sons, it connects us back to Hindu mythology.

The intense posture of strength and balance requires Inhalation. It mainly activates Svadhisthana and Manipura Chakras.

It is a warming and energizing Asana that tones the whole body. It improves balance and strengthens determination in various attempts to succeed in execution.

Yoga Positions with forwarding Flexion

This group of asanas represents surrender and letting go of our idea of ourselves.

Introspective asanas internalize the practice, so they are typically performed at the end of a Yoga session.

## The Yoga Position of the Hero Looking Down (ADHO MUKHA VIRASANA)

A versatile basic posture adapts to various times of practice because of its ability to give refreshment. In addition, it calms the mind and improves breathing.

Full forward bending of the torso stretches the spine. Physiologically requires Exhalation.

A simple exercise, it mainly activates Muladhara and Svadhisthana Chakra energies. It is an excellent Yoga posture for releasing tension and increasing hip openness.

## The Contained Corner Yoga Position (BADDHA KONASANA)

More commonly known as the Butterfly or Cobbler's Yoga Position, Asana starts with an Inhale.

It is a seated Yoga Position that is simple but has remarkable benefits. Energetically it stimulates especially Muladhara, Svadhisthana, and Ajna Chakra. While physically, it improves the function of the abdominal organs, ovaries, prostate, bladder, and kidneys.

Excellent help in relieving PMS, menopausal symptoms, and infertility. Baddha Konasana stretches the inner thigh muscles and groins, proving helpful in facilitating childbirth. Stimulates the heart by improving circulation and regulating blood pressure. It relieves states of anxiety, fatigue, and mild forms of depression and asthma. Restorative yoga pose for flat feet relieves sciatica and relaxes the spine.

## Brahma Yoga Position (BRAHMASANA)

Brahmana takes us back to the Hindu Triad and specifically to Brahma, the Creator.

Yoga Position that stimulates the elemental energies of Muladhara and Svadhisthana Requires the Inhale in its entry.

Mentally relaxing Yoga posture relieves stress, stretches, and lengthens groins, tensor fascia lata, and external rotator muscle.

## The Yoga Posture of the Cow's Muzzle (GOMUKHASANA)

A complete asana, much used in Postural Yoga sequences, Gomukhasana is an excellent shoulder-opening work. It improves breathing.

The Yoga Position requires Inhalation in its entry.

It makes the armpits, arms, hips, and ankles elastic. In addition, it stretches and relaxes the piriformis muscle and buttocks.

Energetically it works predominantly on Muladhara, Svadhisthana, and Anahata.

# The Yoga Position of the Head on the Knee (JANU SIRSASANA)

Yoga posture from full-forward bending of the torso. Physiologically requires Exhalation, which emphasizes the power of surrender.

The rotation of the pelvis mainly stimulates the energies of the Swadhisthana Chakra. It also massages the abdominal organs by toning the liver and kidneys.

Janu Sirsasana is a Postural Position. It corrects imbalances in the spine, such as scoliosis. It promotes mobility of the cox-femoral joint. In addition, it stretches the tendons, buttocks, quadratus lumborum, the low back, and the whole posterior chain of the body.

Refreshing and very relaxing slows heart rate. Calms the mind and relieves tension, states of anxiety, fatigue, and insomnia. Regulates blood pressure and balances the cerebral hemispheres.

# The Yoga Position of the Heron (KROUNCHASANA)

A yoga pose of flexibility and balance, Krounchasana recalls the lightness of a heron.

Asana is active primarily in Svadhisthana and Manipura. Requires Inhalation in its entry.

Benefits include improving balance and lengthening the posterior chains. In addition, stimulates abdominal organs and the heart.

## Turtle Yoga Position (KURMASANA)

Intense Yoga Position. Achieved in the Exhale gives a strong sense of surrender and withdrawal of the reasons. Relaxes on a physical and mental level.

Energetically moves Svadhisthana, the 2nd Chakra. It relaxes the spine and makes the whole-body elastic. Stimulates the intestines by relieving symptoms of constipation and improving digestion. It also acts beneficially on the urogenital system.

## The Yoga Position of Intense Lateral Stretching (PARSVOTTANASANA)

More commonly known as the Pyramid Yoga Position. It is a full-frontal flexion of the torso toward the front leg during Exhalation.

It relaxes the spine by relieving back pain, tension, and stiffness in the leg and hip muscles. Partial balancing posture calms the mind. Improves digestion by massaging abdominal organs. Corrects round and sagging shoulders. Promotes chest opening to benefit good breathing.

Muladhara and Svadhisthana are the main Chakras whose energy is shifted by Parsvottanasana.

## The Yoga Posture of the Reclining Rear Body (PASCIMOTTANASANA)

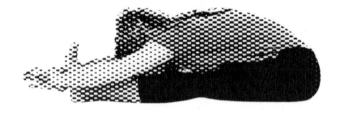

The Hatha Yoga Posture, most commonly known by Clamp to resemble its shape.

Closing Asana. Needs an Exhale to facilitate its abandonment in its entry. Primarily stimulates the energy of the 2nd Chakra, Svadhisthana. It is an introspective Yoga Position that calms the mind and stress resulting in therapeutic for insomnia, sinusitis, and high blood pressure.

It lengthens the spine. It stretches the back of the body. Massages abdominal organs provides relief from issues related to menstrual and menopausal disorders. Stimulates ovaries, uterus, liver, and kidneys.

## Intense Stretching Yoga Position (PRASARITA PADOTTANASANA)

Standing Hatha Yoga posture. Legs spread apart and considerably extended, head and torso bending in the Exhale.

Prasarita Padottanasana stretches tendons and buttocks and, in general, the posterior chains of the legs, strengthening them. It makes the hips and shoulders elastic. It tones the abdominal organs. Lowers blood pressure and calms the mind.

It works mainly on Muladhara, Svadhisthana, and Sahasrara Chakra on an energetic level.

## One-Leg Extension Yoga Position (TRIANG MUKHAIKAPADA PASHIMOTTANASANA)

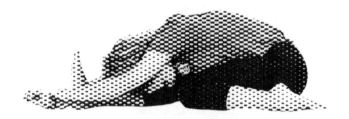

Yoga posture of frontal extension and elongation of the torso. Physiologically requires the Exhale in its entry.

It mainly stimulates the energies of the 1st and 2nd Chakras, Muladhara and Svadhisthana.

Calming and refreshing Asana. Balances the cerebral hemispheres. Massages the abdominal organs. Stretches and lengthens the back of the body, square of the loins, hamstrings, and buttocks. Improves spinal imbalances such as scoliosis.

## The Angle Seated Yoga Posture (UPAVISTA KONASANA)

Seated Yoga posture of surrender in a frontal flexion of the torso in the Exhale allows excellent spinal stretching and opening of the hips while improving circulation in the pelvic area.

Stretches the inner thigh muscles, adductors, and hamstrings, toning the abdominal organs.

An asana that calms the mind on an energetic level works mainly on Muladhara and Swadhisthana, the primary Chakras.

## The Position of Intense Stretching (UTTANASANA)

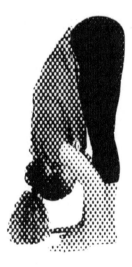

Uttanasana, or Padahastasana "Hands to Feet Position," is commonly known as the Standing Clamp.

Yoga asana with postural benefits relieves sciatica, reduces flat foot, stretches, and strengthens the entire back of the body. In addition, it supports the thighs, knees, and ankles and tones the abdominals while also massaging the internal organs.

On an energetic level, it stimulates Muladhara and Swadhisthana energies.

Introspective Yoga posture stimulates surrender and lowers pressure.

## Yoga Asana in Twist

"Parivritta" Asanas in Twist promote change, purification, and adaptability to various situations in life.

From a physical point of view, Twists squeeze the spine and internal organs of the abdomen by purifying in the Exhale and regenerating in the next Inhale.

The advice is to practice these highly beneficial Yoga Positions consistently and drink enough water to eliminate toxins after practice.

Some of the Asanas we have seen in this article can also be practiced in Twist, adding to the benefits of the position:

Parivritta Ardha Chandrasana, Parivritta Janu Sirsasana, Parivritta Parsvakonasana, Parivritta Trikonasana.

Let's see more.

# The Yoga Posture of the Sage Matsyendra (ARDHA MATSYENDRASANA)

Matsyendra, the Lord of Pisces, is a mythological figure that takes us back to the origins of Hatha Yoga.

While Shiva was telling the mysteries of Yoga to Parvati, a fish listened, captivated enough to learn the Discipline, and transformed into Matsyendra, began to spread Yoga.

Like all the Twists, Ardha Matsyendranasana stimulates and purifies the spine in the Espiro, stretches the buttocks and the piriformis muscle, and relieves asthma.

On an energetic level, it moves the energies of Manipura and Vishudda, digestion, liver, and kidneys.

It promotes change and adaptability to new situations.

# The Rotated Belly Yoga Position (JATHARA PARIVARTANASANA)

A static or dynamic Yoga Asana requires Exhalation to fully enjoy its benefits. It predominantly stimulates Manipura, Anahata, and Vishudda Chakra energies.

It is a Position that balances the sympathetic and parasympathetic nervous systems and relieves tension in the lower back and neck area. In addition, it stretches the outer hip muscle and the oblique abdominal fascia. Finally, it opens the thoracic area improving breathing capabilities. Asana is excellent for constipation, massages internal organs and the spine improving postural issues such as scoliosis.

# Meditation and Relaxation Asana

Some Asanas promote meditation more than others, although every Yoga Position should be meditative in the Presence of self.

Life itself can become a meditation in the ability to embrace the present moment by listening to "That Which Is."

## The Yoga Position of the Corpse (SAVASANA)

Complete surrender at the end of a Hatha Yoga session is the most challenging posture to maintain in transcending the will.

A state of total relaxation of the body and senses in a relaxed mind that lets go of stress and thoughts, allowing contact with inner wisdom.

Exhale facilitates entry into Asana, the body lying supine rooted in the contact points activating and balancing the energies of the 7 Chakras.

Savasana reduces fatigue, lowers blood pressure, relieves headache and fatigue, reduces insomnia, and is suitable for mild depression.

# The Perfect Yoga Position (SIDDHASANA)

It is a reasonably simple Yoga posture from a postural point of view but challenging to maintain in its meditative component.

Siddhasana promotes introspection and withdrawal of the senses.

The still mind in a stable, motionless body rising to the highest Chakras, Ajna, and Sahasrara opening to the more spiritual aspect of the Yoga Discipline.

## Sun Salutation (SURYA NAMASKARA)

In our journey inside the Main Asanas, we could not miss a mention of Surya Namaskara and its benefits.

Better known as Sun Salutation, it is a dynamic sequence consisting of 12 Yoga Asanas, a prayer, spiritual and devotional practice to the primary energy source for life.

It is a comprehensive and energizing Hatha Yoga practice that improves the body's flexibility by summarizing all the benefits of the individual Asanas that comprise it.

# Recommended sequences

## Sequence to relax the mind and make the body more elastic

1. SETU BANDHA SARVANGASANA To reactivate the inner energy
2. PURVOTTANASANA To strengthen the back of the body
3. GARUDASANA For the development of psychophysical balance
4. ANJANEYASANA To stretch the hip flexors
5. BADDHA TRIKONASANA To improve back mobility

# Four Beneficial Yoga Postures

1.  ARDHA CHANDRASANA Half-moon position. An asana that helps bring concreteness and imagination, light and shadow, head and heart together in balance and make us feel completer and more balanced.

2.  PARIVRTTA PARSVAKONASANA. Rotated triangle pose. It is ideal for improving spinal health while promoting more conscious breathing and deep.

3.  NAVASANA Boat position. Strengthens the abdominals, hips, and shoulders; tones the arms; improves coordination, attention, and concentration; and promotes good functioning of internal organs.

4.  UTKATASANA Chair position. It allows you to burn fat and calories quickly; simultaneously, the legs and buttocks strengthen the back, train balance, and correct flat feet.

# Postures to improve your mood

1. ANANDA BALASANA. The posture of the happy child. The posture involves a complete relaxation of the back muscles. In addition, it calms the brain and mind.

2. MALASANA. The posture of the garland. Malasana promotes calmness, and stability and, at the same time, improves grounding, which is essential for having more excellent balance mental and physical.

3. ASHWA SANCHALANASANA. The equestrian posture. It helps to improve self-esteem and open up to the outside world by opening the heart upward on an emotional level.

4. UTTHAN PRISTHASANA. The lizard pose. The posture stimulates metabolism, provides energy, and relieves anxiety.

5. VRKSASANA. The tree posture. The tree posture strengthens the body's limbs and promotes balance and concentration.

# Yoga Poses for the Chakras

1. BALASANA. It roots you and brings peace. It calms the mind and instills confidence in yourself and in life.

2. EKA PADA RAJAKAPOTASANA. Increases creativity and inspiration, releasing stress, trauma, fears, and anxieties. It helps you flow with life.

3. KAKASANA. Connects you with your personal power and increases self-esteem and inner clarity. Improves digestion of food and life experiences.

4. URDHVA DHANURASANA. Opens you to the beauty and magic of life. Frees the breath. Opens the heart to the energy of love and forgiveness.

5. SARVANGASANA. Stimulates the thyroid gland and brings energy to the throat, promoting authentic expression and communication. Helps you let go of "negative" thoughts.

6. URDHVA PRASARITA EKA PADASANA. Helps you let go of excess mental energy and increases intuition. It purifies the whole system and makes the mind accessible and spacious.

7. SIRSHASANA. Relaxes and strengthens the brain, preventing headaches. Stimulates the lymphatic system and helps remove toxins. Brings peace, enlightenment, and unity to you.

# Postures to reduce anxiety

1. ANANDAMADIRASANA. Simple asana to begin to calm the mind and nervous system.

2. SHASHANKASANA. Asana relieves pressure on the intervertebral discs, improving the quality of nerve connections branching from the spinal cord.

3. BHUJANGASANA. Asana stimulates all nerve activity in the body, which passes through the spine.

4. ADHO MUKHA SVANASANA. General nerve toning.

5. DANDASANA. Primary stimulation of the central nervous system.

6. VIPARITA KARANI ASANA. Thyroid stimulation and rebalancing of the nervous, circulatory, endocrine, and respiratory systems. Stimulation of abdominal breathing is helpful in relieving stress

7. SHALABHASANA. Stimulation of the nervous system, particularly in the lower abdomen and solar plexus, is often an area of deep anxiety buildup.

8. PASHIMOTTANASANA. Complete decongestion of the solar plexus, which drives away any anxious state

# Poses to combat Insomnia

1.  SUKASANA. Leaning back in the chair. Simple cross-legged posture Excellent introduction to the restorative sequence. This posture begins the relaxation process, calms the agitated mind, and relaxes abdominal tension.

2.  VIPARITA KARANI. Simple variation. Inverted posture with legs in support. This simple restorative inversion is the queen of stress relievers, promoting relaxation, reducing fatigue, calming the nervous system, and producing a sense of calm and balance.

3.  SUPPORTED SAVASANA. Relaxation posture with supports. Ideal for completing the restorative sequence, this supported position eliminates the last muscle tension, balances the nervous system, and accompanies you to experience the stillness of mind.

# Postures to combat back pain

1. TADASANA. The mountain pose. Simple asana to begin to calm the mind and nervous system.

2. UTTHITA TRIKONASANA. Triangle pose. Asana relieves pressure on the intervertebral discs, improving the quality of nerve connections branching from the spinal cord.

3. ASHWA SANACHALASANA. The equestrian posture. Stretches the Ileo - psoas by promoting proper posture of the vertebral spine. The buttocks, while increasing their elasticity, are toned.

4. KUMBHASANA/PHALANKASANA. the plank position. Tones the upper limbs, shoulders, and abdomen, responsible along with many other muscles, for the correct posture of the upper body.

5. ADHO MUKHA SVANASANA/MERUASANA. Upside-down dog yoga pose. Goes to distance the vertebrae by giving more space to the intervertebral discs. This leads to more excellent elasticity of the spine and promotes better mobility of the pelvis.

6. UTTANASANA. Standing forward, bend. Stretches and strengthens the muscles of the lower limbs, back, neck and shoulders, leading to the progressive anthro-posterior release of the pelvis.

7. MANDUKASANA. The frog posture. Goes to relieves all tension in the lumbar spine and increases the space between vertebral bodies to benefit the discs.

# Conclusion

Thank you for coming this far. My goal is to spread the culture of Yoga with its theory but, more importantly, with its practice.

Remember that it does not matter how much time you devote to Yoga. Still, instead, it is essential to have quality sessions. Once you get the routine right, it only takes a few minutes a day to feel great about your body and mind.

The nuances of Yoga are endless; the interpretations that each of us gives to movement, balance, and all the more or less complex postures allow us to perceive how our body can change its internal forces and energies to feel better and live a life without stress and anxiety.

Suppose you enjoyed this book, its contents, and all its illustrations. In that case, I strongly encourage you to leave a positive review on Amazon. Frame this QR code with your smartphone, and you will be redirected directly to the Amazon page.

If you intend to contact me privately instead, please email me at this

**yogaevans@outlook.com**

Happy Yoga and good luck.

*Viola Evans*

Printed in Great Britain
by Amazon

86969471R00068